Contents

	1.	Start the show	4	Violin
	3.	Heat haze	6	Violin/Viola
	4.	Medieval tale	7	Violin/Viola
*	4.	Medieval tale	8	Viola
	5.	Cornish May song	9	Violin/Viola
*	5.	In memory	10	Viola
	6.	Chase in the dark	11	Violin/Viola
	7.	Merrily danced the Quaker's wife	12	Violin/Viola
	7.	Merrily danced the Quaker's wife	13	Viola
	9.	Jingle bells (J. Pierpont)	14	Violin/Viola
	10.	Allegretto in G (Mozart)	16	Violin/Viola
	10.	Allegretto in C (Mozart)	17	Viola
	11.	Pick a bale of cotton	18	Violin/Viola
	13.	Finale from the 'Water Music' (Handel)	19	Violin/Viola
	13.	Finale from the 'Water Music' (Handel)	20	Viola
	14.	Ecossaise in G (Beethoven)	21	Violin/Viola
	15.	Fiddle/Viola Time rag	22	Violin/Viola
	16.	Playing on the ol' banjo	24	Violin/Viola
*	17.	On the go!	25	Violin/Viola
	18.	Yodelling song	26	Violin/Viola
*	18.	Blue whale	27	Viola
	19.	Takin' it easy	28	Violin/Viola
	20.	Gypsy dance	30	Violin/Viola
*	20.	Mean street chase	31	Viola
	22.	I got those fiddle/viola blues	32	Violin/Viola
	23.	Air in G (J. C. Bach)	34	Violin/Viola
	23.	Air in C (J. C. Bach)	35	Viola
	24.	Prelude from 'Te Deum' (Charpentier)	36	Violin/Viola
	24.	Prelude from 'Te Deum' (Charpentier)	37	Viola
*	25.	That's how it goes!	38	Violin/Viola
	26.	Flamenco dance	40	Violin/Viola
	27.	Somebody's knocking at your door	42	Violin/Viola
	28.	The old chariot	43	Violin/Viola
	28.	The old chariot	46	Viola
	29.	Adam in the garden	44	Violin/Viola
	30.	Air (Handel)	47	Violin/Viola
	31.	The wee cooper o' Fife	48	Violin/Viola
	32.	Aerobics!	50	Violin/Viola
*	32.	Aerobics!	51	Viola
	33.	Caribbean sunshine	52	Violin/Viola

* These pieces are compatible with *Cello Time Runners* or *Sprinters* (In memory).

Violin/Viola

1. Start the show

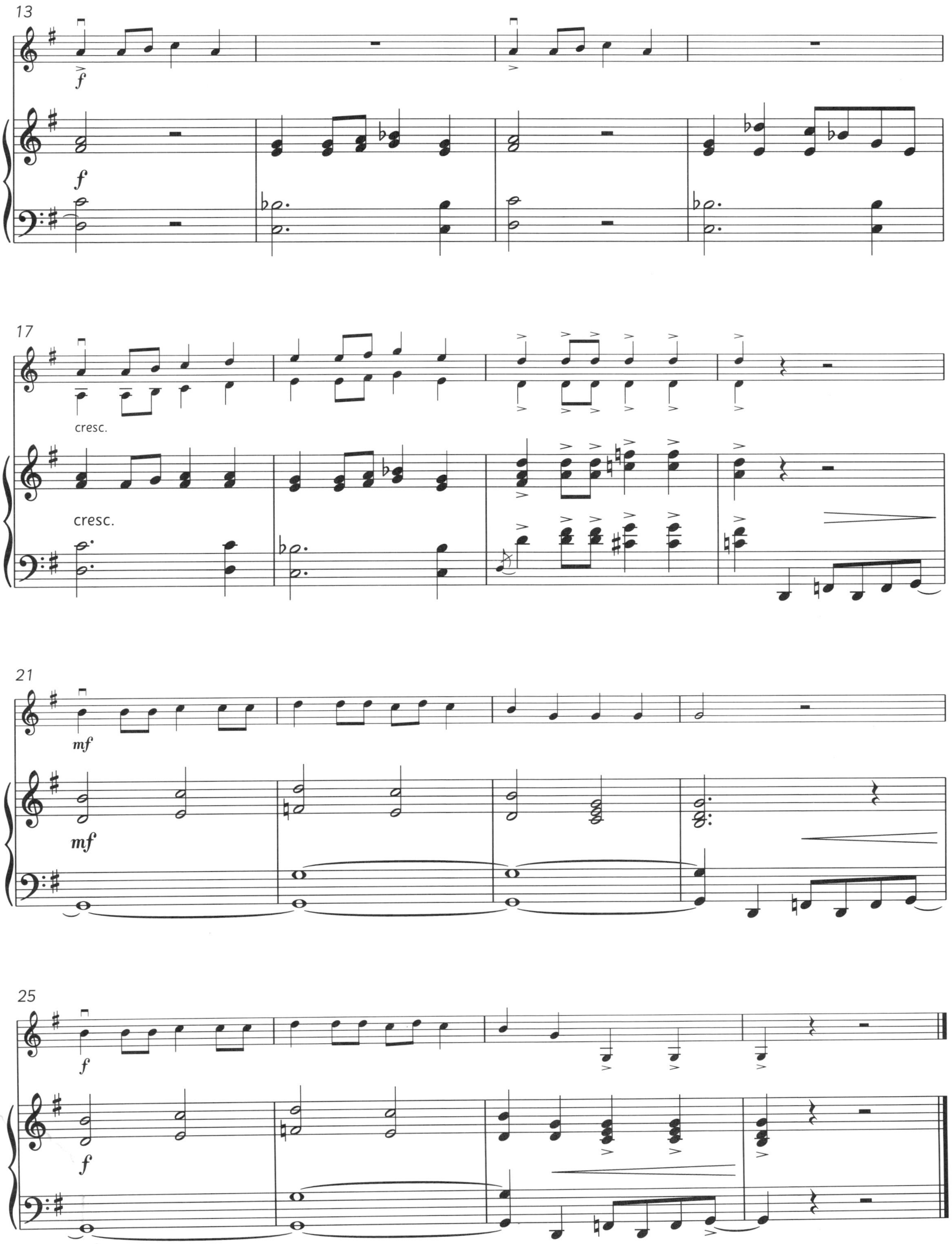
13
f
f
17
cresc.
cresc.
21
mf
mf
25
f
f

3. Heat haze

4. Medieval tale

4. Medieval tale

5. Cornish May song

Traditional

5. In memory

for Eileen

6. Chase in the dark

7. Merrily danced the Quaker's wife

Scottish

7. Merrily danced the Quaker's wife

Scottish

14 Violin/Viola

9. Jingle bells

J. Pierpont

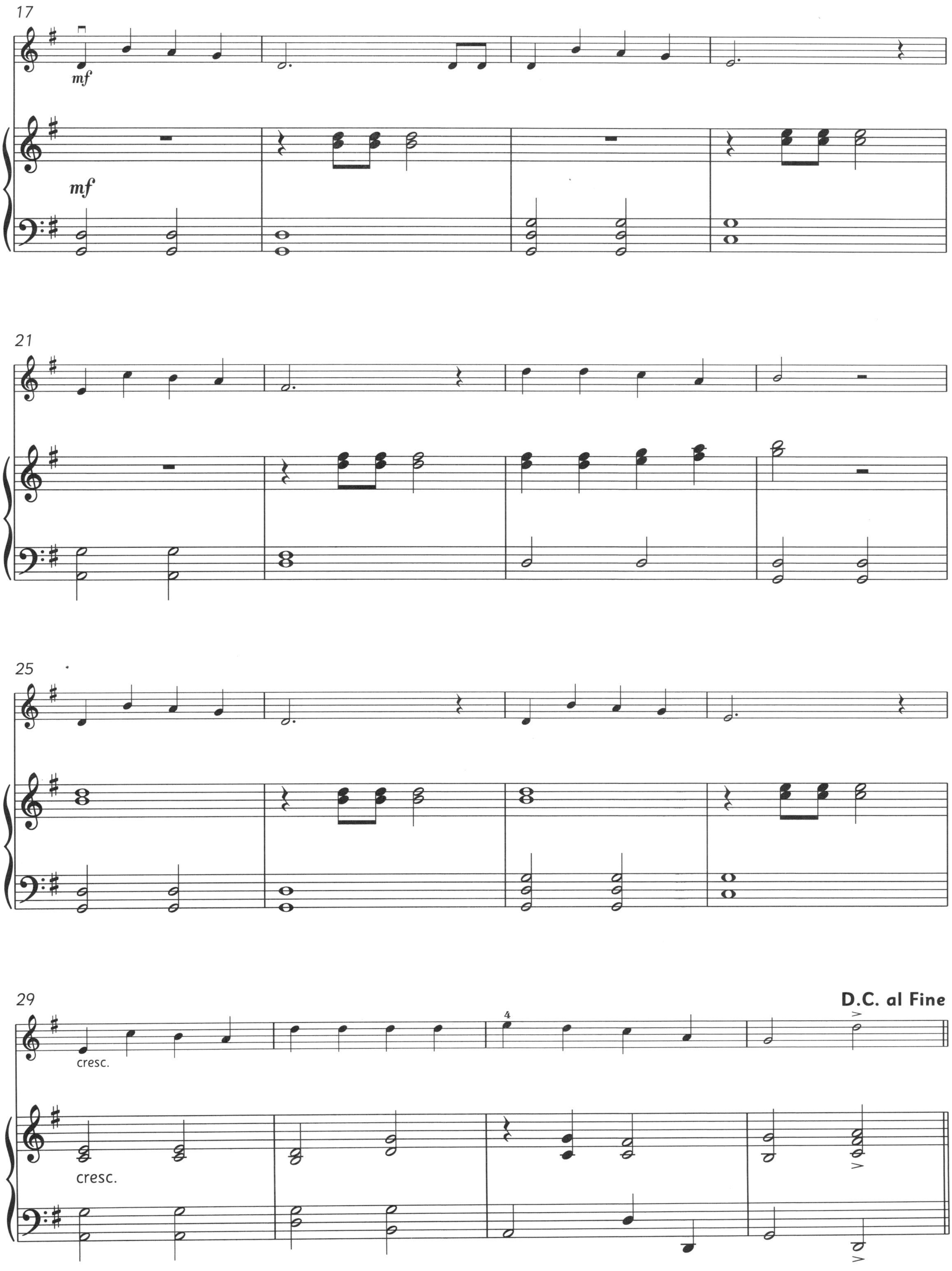
17
mf
mf
21
25
29
D.C. al Fine
cresc.
cresc.

10. Allegretto in G

Mozart

10. Allegretto in C

Mozart

11. Pick a bale of cotton

American

13. Finale from the 'Water Music'

Handel

13. Finale from the 'Water Music'

Handel

14. Ecossaise in G

Beethoven

Violin solo: piano part as written; viola solo: play violin part in right hand bars 5–8 and 13–16; violin–viola duet: piano part as written.

15. Fiddle/Viola Time rag

Violin/Viola

16. Playing on the ol' banjo

Traditional

17. On the go!

* The repeat is written out in full in the violin and viola parts.

18. Yodelling song

Traditional

18. Blue whale

19. Takin' it easy

*The repeat is written out in full in the violin and viola parts.

Violin/Viola

20. Gypsy dance

20. Mean street chase

22. I got those fiddle/viola blues

Violin/Viola

23. Air in G

J. C. Bach

23. Air in C

J. C. Bach

24. Prelude from 'Te Deum'

Charpentier

24. Prelude from 'Te Deum'

Charpentier

25. That's how it goes!

Violin/Viola 39

26. Flamenco dance

Violin/Viola 41

27. Somebody's knocking at your door

Traditional

28. The old chariot

Sea shanty

29. Adam in the garden

Jamaican

Relaxed tempo

Nos. 29 and 28 (viola) are reversed to avoid a page turn.

Violin/Viola

28. The old chariot

Sea shanty

30. Air

(Violin duet with viola ensemble part)

Handel

*Play these notes if the second violin part isn't played.

31. The wee cooper o' Fife

Scottish

Violin/Viola

32. Aerobics!

32. Aerobics!

33. Caribbean sunshine